Junior High's a Jungle, Lord

CLAIR G. COSBY

HERALD PRESS
Scottdale, Pennsylvania
Kitchener, Ontario
1988

Library of Congress Cataloging-in-Publication Data

Cosby, Clair G., 1944-
    Junior high's a jungle, Lord/Clair G. Cosby.
        p.   cm.
    Summary: Presents a sequence of prayers and devotional readings
concerning the difficulties of leaving elementary school and
adjusting to the demands of junior high school.
    ISBN 0-8361-3455-9 (pbk.)
    1. Youth—Prayer-books and devotions—English.   2. Junior high
school students—Prayer-books and devotions—English.   [1. Prayer
books and devotions.   2. Student adjustment.   3. Conduct of life.
4. Christian life.]   I. Title.
BV4531.2.C66 1988
242'.63—dc19   87-27040
                                                                    CIP
                                                                    AC

Scripture quotations are from *The New English Bible*. © The
Delegates of the Oxford University Press and The Syndics of the
Cambridge University Press 1961, 1970. Reprinted by permission.

JUNIOR HIGH'S A JUNGLE, LORD
Copyright © 1988 by Herald Press, Scottdale, Pa. 15683
        Published simultaneously in Canada by Herald Press,
        Kitchener, Ont. N2G 4M5. All rights reserved.
Library of Congress Catalog Card Number: 87-27040
International Standard Book Number: 0-8361-3455-9
Printed in the United States of America
Design by Gwen Stamm/Cover photo by Jan Doyle

92 91 90 89 88 10 9 8 7 6 5 4 3 2 1

*To Sarah,
Sallie, and James.*

Contents

June: Matthew 5:3-10

My monthly prayer diary: Matthew 6:6

♦♦♦

Getting through the jungle

Does changing from elementary school to junior high have to be terrible? Does everyone feel a little bit scared of forgetting locker combinations and not getting to class on time? What if you lose your lunch money and can't call home? What if no one saves you a seat in the cafeteria? What if none of your friends are in your classes?

And once the first month or so of school is over, does everyone go through that time of feeling like a nobody who doesn't belong? Do other kids get hassled at home about practicing piano or needing a haircut or finishing homework in time for choir?

I believe that most adolescents go through times when junior high is scary and friends let them down. When parents and teachers don't seem to understand and school seems like a jungle, most young people wonder at times if it wouldn't really be easier not to grow up.

Through all these days of change inside yourself and confusion all around you, there is one person who will always remain steady and faithful to you: God. It is to God that you can turn when the school bus doesn't stop because you look too young or you fall on the stairs in front of five ninth-graders. God rejoices with you when your story gets into the school newspaper. He cares in those moments when you feel like a nobody.

God wants you to share with him when you are worried about your homework, angry about the language you hear in the halls, excited about the state math contest.

Everything in your life that is important to you is important to God. You can talk to him in prayer wherever you are, whenever you want. He is always there with you.

This book of prayers moves through the school year (from September through June) as one young person talks over daily happenings with God. There is a month by-month section in the back of the book for you to write your own prayer concerns. Your Monthly Prayer Diary will help you remember the things you have shared with God during this growing up, changing time from elementary to junior high school.

Remember, God wants to share your life with you—the problems and worries and the special good feelings. You can talk to him in prayer wherever you are, whenever you want. God is always there with you.

Clair Cosby
Burke, Virginia

◆◆◆

Set your mind on God's kingdom and his justice before everything else, and all the rest will come to you as well. So do not be anxious about tomorrow; tomorrow will look after itself. Each day has troubles enough of its own.

—Matthew 6:33-34

SEPTEMBER . . .

◆◆◆

Lord, how will I carry so many books?

Mom and I went to pay book fees at the junior high today. We walked through my schedule of classes, and talked to the teachers who were in their rooms. In each room there were stacks of textbooks. Six classes—two books for some of the subjects. I'll need separate loose-leaf notebooks for two of my teachers, too.

My homeroom teacher said we could only go to our lockers at the beginning of the day, at lunchtime, and at bus call. How can I carry so many books around with me?

Junior high school students don't carry book bags or backpacks, or I guess they don't. What do they do? I don't want to look like some little lost sixth-grader who doesn't know what to do next Monday.

Oh, I wish that I had looked around at the other kids in the halls when we came over for that orientation meeting last spring. I just didn't notice what they were holding. I was so excited about changing schools and changing classes that I forgot the simple things like carrying books.

Lord, help me not to look foolish the first day. Help me know what to do with all of those books. It's the silly details about junior high life that have me worried. I want so much to fit in at my new school.

◆◆◆

What shall I wear the first day, Lord?

I don't want to look too dressed up on Monday. That's what the elementary kids do—their mothers all get them a special dress or outfit for the first day of school. I want to look nice but sort of casual, you know.

Do you think I should wear jeans? All of the kids were wearing jeans when we visited last year—but it was pretty cool the day we went on the tour of the junior high. Maybe they wear shorts on the first day. My mom probably won't let me do that.

I know that clothes aren't all that important to you. I know that you would just want me to dress "appropriately" to make you and my parents proud of me.

But I want to look like the other kids too. I want to blend in. I want them not to notice me because I look wrong in some way.

Is it bad to want to be like the others, Lord? I promise you that deep down inside I'll be the person you want me to be. I promise that I will act as you want me to act. But help me think of what to wear so that the other kids will accept me. You understand, don't you? Everybody needs to belong.

Lord, will I be able to get to class on time?

The other day when Mom and I walked around the school we had a lot of time. We found all of the rooms on my schedule. Most of my classes were pretty close together. I guess the counselors try to do that for the seventh-graders.

But orchestra, Lord! Orchestra is all the way on the wrong side of the building from my other classes—and downstairs.

Four minutes is not very long. Why don't they give us more time to get to class? I really don't think that I can make it across the building that fast.

There will be masses of people in those halls. There are hundreds of students in my new school. It must be terrible when you aren't sure where you are going and then have all those other kids pushing around you going to their own classes.

I know that you can help me do a lot of things, Lord. You won't pull magic tricks, but you can help me solve problems. How will I get to orchestra on time?

Please help me get to the right classrooms at the right time. Help me to stop worrying so much about the first day of school. I know I'm acting like nobody else ever went to junior high—but *I* never did, and I'm scared.

◆◆◆

The school bus didn't stop for me, Lord

It seemed like the bus took forever coming. Finally I saw it rounding the corner. I stepped to the edge of the curb with a smile on my face—and the bus never stopped. It didn't even slow down. It was like I was invisible or something.

I couldn't believe it. There went the bus on down the street and around the corner out of sight!

I guess I just stood there for a minute. Dad had been watching from the house to make sure I got on the bus. It's a good thing he hadn't left for work yet, or I would have missed the first day.

The worst part of all was the bus driver apologizing after school in front of half a busload of kids. He said he hadn't realized I was a junior high student when he saw me standing in front of the house. *He thought I looked too young to be in junior high!*

I was angry and embarrassed. I just tucked my head and went to sit in the first empty seat. I didn't say anything to anyone.

Lord, I don't know how I'll face those kids on the bus tomorrow. I really want to ask Dad to take me to school again. Help me have the courage to get on the bus in the morning just like nothing went wrong today.

Lord, what IS my locker combination?

I can't believe the dumb thing that I did at bus call this afternoon! There were so many people moving through the hall around my locker, and there was so much noise. It was muggy and hot, and I was afraid I might be late to the bus and not have a way home.

I just could not think of my locker combination. I stood there in the hall trying to force myself to calm down and think logically . . . and I just couldn't.

So here I am at home in my room with all the books from my afternoon classes and none from my morning ones. I don't have homework in some of the books I brought home. I need that history textbook and notebook back at school in my locker to finish the definitions my teacher assigned for tomorrow.

How do I walk up to her and say: "I would have done my homework, Miss Morris, but I forgot my locker combination after school yesterday." That ranks with the excuse, "A dog ran off with my paper when I dropped it at the bus stop."

Lord, I know that you can keep me calm if I just rely on you. I know that you can help me get that locker opened anytime I need to. Please help me to remember you're with me in the middle of a crowded school hallway as much as when we're talking alone together here in my room.

I lost my shoe
on the "down" staircase, Lord

It was because of my own vanity. I didn't want to wear my sneakers today because I wanted to look special for school pictures . . . I know, they weren't taking pictures of my feet.

I decided to wear my church shoes, and they were just a little too large. I was in a hurry to get to third period class and was going down the stairs too fast.

Then—all at once—there I was on the bottom step with my books all over the floor and my shoe in the hand of a ninth-grade boy. Five ninth-graders were standing all around me. I was so embarrassed.

They were really nice to help me, but I was holding up all of the other kids on the stairs and making such a spectacle of myself. I wanted to melt right into the crowd and disappear.

But, no! The boy who found my shoe insisted that he walk me to class. He teased me and said he was making sure I didn't get knocked down on the way.

Lord, I'd love to be noticed by a ninth-grade boy if it was for something neat I'd done—not falling down the stairs! I felt so dumb and clumsy and mad at myself for wearing shoes I knew were too big just because I thought they looked better. I hope you'll help me remember to be more sensible next time. I hope I'll listen to you.

Lord, they saved me a seat in the cafeteria

You know how sometimes I am not so sure that my friends like me. Sometimes I think that they just put up with me because I'm Debbie's friend.

Well, today I had to stay and talk to my English teacher about his story assignment before I went to my locker and the cafeteria at lunchtime. I was so late getting downstairs that the lines were almost short.

The tables looked full already. When I started walking down the window side of the cafeteria, looking around for an empty space, Cindy and her friends waved for me to come over to their table. They had saved me a seat.

They wanted to know what had taken so long. They were interested in what Mr. Williams told me. They listened.

It made me feel so good that they do care about me. I felt good all afternoon because they wanted me to be with them at lunch.

Help me to show them that I want to be their friend too. Help me not to be so shy about sitting next to new people and talking to them. Lord, I really want to make friends.

I have friends in all my classes, Lord

There are five elementary schools sending kids to my junior high. I was worried that I wouldn't even see my friends from last year—but I see people I know all day long in the halls, in class, and at lunch.

It would be nice if Debbie were in all of my classes, but she takes p.e. in the morning and art instead of orchestra. We have different English and science periods too. Cindy's in my math class, and I know lots of people in history.

A few days ago in English class I talked with two girls who like to read mystery stories just like I do. We're going to trade some books around. History's hard, but some of us study together in the morning before homeroom. It's nice having classes with so many different kids each day.

It would be hard to come in as a new student in school and not know *anybody* at all. I'm glad I have old friends in all my classes, Lord, but help me to make some new friends too. Help me to look for the kids who don't seem to know anybody. They need friends even more than I do, and I can be their friend.

How will I ever do all this homework, Lord?

Who do they think we are—super brains? Do they think we like to work five hours a night on homework just because we've reached the magic land of junior high? It makes me sick! Somebody ought to stand up and tell them what they're doing to us!

I cannot believe that three of my teachers have assigned tests on the same night that dear Miss Morris decided we needed to write fifteen history definitions. I just can't believe it.

I know that I can't get all of this work done, and I refuse to do it! It is unreasonable, and they are just going to have to take what they get tomorrow.

It takes me twenty minutes to write a history definition. I have fifteen to do. That makes 20×15 . . . that's 300 minutes . . . that's five hours. *Five hours!* Can you believe it? She must be crazy.

It's 4:00 now. I can't get those definitions done before 9:00 even if I don't eat supper—and then there are those three tests! It seems like junior highs should coordinate their test days. If I were running things, I wouldn't allow more than two periods a day to test. Teachers could have tests on Monday, Wednesday, and Friday—two periods a day. Now *that's* a terrific idea, but it doesn't help me tonight.

Lord, please help me budget my time. Help me remember all these facts I've been studying. I really want to do my work, but sometimes the teachers are unfair.

Thanks for being there with me, Lord

Most of my friends would not understand how I feel, but you know how good it is to share. I know that no matter how hard the day is—or how good it is—you are there with me.

In a way, you're more of my best friend than Debbie is. I mean she and I have been in school together for five years. We've talked on the phone, played together, spent nights together . . . but in some ways I can't share who I really am with anyone but you.

I guess it's partly because I know there isn't anything I can't say to you . . . and that anything I do say to you is just between us. You really understand. It's like you're right there beside me all the time rooting me on, wanting me to be the best that I can be.

I love my parents, Lord, but they can't go to school with me. I love my friends, but they don't always care about me. I love you, Lord, best of all. Thanks for just being you and loving me for just being me.

◆◆◆

*A*sk, and you will receive; seek, and you will find; knock, and the door will be opened. For everyone who asks receives, he who seeks finds, and to him who knocks, the door will be opened.

—Matthew 7:7-8

DECEMBER . . .

I can't take my cello on the school bus, Lord

Dad's on a trip this week, so I brought my cello home on the bus this afternoon. I never want to ride that bus again!

I had a hard time bringing the bagful of books for homework *and* the cello, but I did manage to drag it all onto the bus. I found a seat halfway down the aisle and put my books down, but the cello wouldn't fit between the seats.

While I was trying to get my cello and books and myself situated, the boy behind me started making remarks: "Why doesn't a shrimpy girl like you play violin? Who are you hiding in that big brown bag, little girl? Your fiddle sure has a good figure, honey. . . ."

I was so mad I wanted to hit him, but I just sat very straight and looked in front of me, trying to ignore him.

Then we were at my bus stop. I tried to hurry while all along that boy kept making remarks. My cello got stuck between the seats. I was afraid I'd break it if I jerked too hard. I just couldn't get it loose. The bus driver had to come help me.

So you see, I'm not just being dramatic, Lord. The bus driver said that my cello was causing problems and I can't take it on the bus anymore. What am I going to do, Lord? What am I going to do?

♦♦♦

Should I do my homework, Lord, or go to choir?

My parents have always told me that I should be a "responsible" member of any group that I join. I shouldn't call myself a member if I'm not willing to make the sacrifices to be reliable.

I know that our youth choir is singing special music next Sunday, and I know that my director is counting on me to be there. But I have math and history and science homework tonight. It's not like I had some sort of long assignment that I've been putting off till the last minute. All of these are things my teachers decided to give me to do today.

How shall I decide what to do, Lord? I want to serve you in my church, and I want to do my best at school.

I might have time to do homework *and* go to choir, but how do I know if I will? Choir is from 6:30 to 8:00. What if I do some homework, eat supper, go to choir, and when I come home there isn't enough time left to finish my assignments?

I wish my parents would decide things like this for me. They say I have to make up my own mind because they don't know how long it will take me to do the work. Well, I don't either.

Will you think I don't love you, Lord, if I stay home tonight? Will the choir director understand? Will the other kids think I'm irresponsible if I'm not at practice?

Lord, my story is going into the school newspaper

Mr. Williams asked me to stay after class again to-day, and guess what? He has submitted my story about the girl basketball star to the school newspaper . . . and they like it too!

I'm going to be in print!

I still can't believe it. I don't think I will until I actually see it in the newspaper.

I was going to be quiet about the whole thing and not tell anyone until they saw it next week. Then I'd act sort of surprised that they made a big deal about it.

But I couldn't wait!

When I got to the cafeteria, the girls at the table wanted to know why I had to stay late in English, and I just had to tell them the good news.

Of course, they don't understand how excited I am. I still don't know exactly how I feel except that I do feel special.

Thank you, Lord, for giving me the talent to write. Thank you for giving my teacher the idea to submit my story. It was a wonderful surprise.

She likes Cindy better than me, Lord

I really knew it already. Whenever I have invited Debbie over lately she already has made plans to have Cindy over to her house or to do something with her.

I honestly don't know how it happened.

It doesn't seem fair. Debbie has been my best friend for five years. Doesn't she have any loyalty? I have notes and cards she's written to me over the years. She's told me over and over again that she'll always be my best friend. "True friends forever—nothing can part us!"

Hah . . . so much for true friendship!

I guess I shouldn't have asked her right out, "Do you like Cindy more than me?" I was secretly hoping that she would say, "Of course not. You'll always be my best friend."

But she didn't say that. She said, "Yes, I do like Cindy better than you. I never did like you in the first place."

That hurt me, Lord. It was bad enough that I lost my best friend, but she sort of took away my best memories too. She probably didn't mean it. She was just mad I had asked her . . . but I sure am feeling down.

What did I do wrong, Lord? Is there something wrong with me that I can't keep a friend? Will you help me figure it out?

There isn't any time to stare at the ceiling, Lord

If anyone had asked me a few weeks ago what was the worst thing about junior high, I might have said, "Taking showers in p.e.," or "Having to remember your locker combination," or "Getting through the cafeteria line in 30 minutes," but I think I've finally figured it out.

I can't remember ever in my life being too busy to sit for a half hour in the tree house playing with my cat, or to cuddle up with a good mystery book for an hour in the window seat, or to lie on my bed and stare at the ceiling.

Where does all my time go?

I do homework. I help with the dishes and feed the cats. I practice piano and cello. I go to youth group and youth choir and church services. And the time is all gone. I've even stopped soaking in the bathtub because showers are faster.

Maybe I'm just not organized yet, but I wish you would help me, Lord. Everybody needs some part of their lives that isn't already scheduled. I miss that time staring at the ceiling and thinking about things.

I've been asked to take a statewide math test, Lord!

I am so excited I could pop! We're going to take a bus to the community college thirty miles away next Saturday. There will be fifty of us going from our entire county —only fifty!

I've never been to a college campus, and we're going to be there all day—even eat lunch in the student union building.

I don't exactly know what the test is about or why we are taking it. My math teacher just picked a few of us, and Mom said I could go.

Isn't that terrific!

I know that I do very well in math, but this must mean that I have a special math ability. It's good to hear good things about myself every once in a while, Lord.

Sometimes I feel so dumb and out of it. Sometimes I wonder why you made me like I am. But today I feel smart and special and proud—and thankful to you for myself.

◆◆◆

I'll never play piano like my sister, Lord

There she goes again ... into the living room to practice. She's two years younger than I am, but she plays piano better than I do.

I could be better—if I only had the free time she does.

She never seems to have any homework, or if she does, it only takes her an hour or so. Just wait till she gets to junior high. She'll have so much homework that she won't have practice time either.

Oh, I sound mighty jealous, don't I, Lord?

It's not all jealousy, you know. I really would like to play piano like my sister does. She makes it look so easy when she sits down to try out a new piece. I know that it comes from practicing so hard as well as from having a gift for music.

I guess I'm sort of sad, too, because I feel like I'll never have the time to get much better at piano than I already am. It's like the closing chapter of a book already, and I'm only in seventh grade!

Help me not to be so pessimistic, Lord. Help me to find a few minutes every day to practice piano. Maybe I'll never be as good at playing as my sister, but that doesn't mean I have to give up altogether.

Lord, I'm a nobody

The principal passed me in the hall this morning and smiled, but he doesn't know my name. The librarian sees me every week at least and has helped me on re search for a science project, but she doesn't know who I am. The bus driver knows I'm the girl who got the cello stuck between the seats and where my house is, but he probably hasn't heard my name.

I'm a nobody here.

Last year the principal and secretary and custodians and librarian and cafeteria workers all knew my name. I'd carry a note to the office for my teacher, and some-one would smile and say, "Thank you, Emily."

But it's not just my name, Lord. It's ME no one knows here. My teachers all have over a hundred students. They see us for less than an hour a day, and we all must seem to be a big blur to them.

Oh, there are a few students they know—the athletes, the cheerleaders, the presidents of the clubs, the kids with the best grades and worst behavior—but there are hundreds of us, Lord—a few somebodies and hundreds of nobodies.

I know that you made each of us special. There is no one exactly like me in the world. Thank you for loving me as if I were your only child—for loving each of us that way. Help me never to treat someone else like a nobody, Lord. It's so easy to feel you're a nobody without even trying.

I can't stand the language in the halls, Lord

I s there something that happens to kids when they turn 12 or 13 that makes them want to try out bad language, Lord? I hear it everywhere at school—the halls, the cafeteria, the bus, and even in the classroom when the teacher isn't listening.

It makes me so angry because I can't seem to get away from it.

Even some kids that I really like in lots of ways don't seem to care what comes out of their mouth.

Mom says that people who use profanity are not smart enough to think of the right word to use, but I see smart kids using those same ugly words.

Are they trying to show off to each other? Are they trying to shock their parents? Or do they just not think anything about what they say?

I hate to hear such ugliness coming out of so many mouths. I feel like there isn't anyone to have a decent conversation with at school.

Lord, should I still make friends with people who use profanity? Jesus hung around with some pretty bad people without becoming like them. They became more like him.

Am I a good enough example to make a difference to other kids, or should I just stay away from them? I don't want to get so used to profanity, Lord, that it doesn't bother me anymore.

"We are the Tigers!"

We had our first basketball game today, Lord. It was so much fun. The gymnasium was full of kids and parents.

Our whole crowd was yelling, "We are the Tigers—T-I-G-E-R-S—TIGERS!" It was the first time that I really felt like I was part of the school.

I really belong to the school!

It's a good feeling to know that there are hundreds of people watching a game in one place who all belong to each other in some way. We are different, sometimes think and act differently, but we belong to each other.

The gym got sticky hot, the noise was ringing in our ears, and the benches were hard. But we were laughing and calling to each other when we left the school and walked through the parking lot.

Wouldn't it be wonderful, Lord, if something could bring all the earth's people together like that?

You created us all. You want us to be brothers and sisters. But so often we notice how different we are from one another instead of how alike we are.

It must make you sad when we can't enjoy living together in this beautiful world you made for us. I hope you'll help my friends and me to make the world better and more loving—a place where everybody belongs to each other and to you.

◆◆◆

Y ou are light for all the world. A town that stands on a hill cannot be hidden. When a lamp is lit, it is not put under the meal-tub, but on the lamp-stand, where it gives light to everyone in the house. And you, like the lamp, must shed light among your fellows, so that, when they see the good you do, they may give praise to your Father in heaven.

—Matthew 5:14-16

M A R C H . . .

Doesn't anyone else care about studying, Lord?

E nglish class was the pits today. Well, not exactly that bad. It's just that I'm the only one who ever raises her hand to answer a question.

The other kids don't bother answering questions when the teacher tries to discuss what we've read, so I try to help the teacher out. Well, usually I just get interested in what Mr. Williams is saying, and I want to share what I think too.

I've decided the other kids aren't shy. They just haven't read the material or done the homework. They think it's smart to let me study and answer questions while they sit back and wait for the bell to ring.

You know all of the kids aren't like that, but so many of them don't seem to care at all in most of my classes.

How can they not want to learn? I don't understand them. They probably can't understand me either, so I guess we're even. There's just so much to find out about in the world, and I want to know all that I can.

There are times when they tease me, when they get irritated because I have so much to say. But deep down I don't think they care one way or another.

I'm sad for my friends, Lord. They are missing so much, and they don't even know it. They think they're being smart to get out of work, but how will they know what to do with their lives? I'm worried about them.

I like my hair long, Lord

If she mentions haircut to me once more this week, I may run into my room screaming!

Why is my mother always wanting to tell me how to run my life? My hair is my own. It isn't bothering her—she doesn't have to wash and comb and curl it. She doesn't have to wear it around on her head!

When I was a child, she had a right to take me for haircuts. She even washed my hair and dryed it for me. I don't need her help any more. I can take care of my own hair, and I can make my own decisions.

She says she just wants me to get the ends trimmed. Ha! I know what will happen when we get to the shop. First, she'll casually point out the styling books in the waiting room. She'll flip through and find all of the haircuts she thinks will look nice on me. Then, she'll ask the stylist if she doesn't agree—teamwork—let's convince the stubborn little girl to do what mother wants.

I won't even go with her for a trim because I don't want the hassle.

I don't care what others think. If people don't like my hair the way I want to fix it, that's their problem. They can't be very good friends if they want to change me.

Lord, I wish you would make my mother see that I'm growing up and don't need her advice about *everything* anymore. I'll still ask her about the hard decisions, but can't she let me decide some things for myself?

Patty loaned me lunch money, Lord

I didn't realize I'd forgotten my money until I was going down the hall to the cafeteria. I felt in my pocket and remembered leaving the change on the counter when I ran for my bus this morning.

Well, hunger isn't so terrible if you know that you'll be home in four hours anyway. I went on to the table and sat down to wait for the other girls.

Patty was the first one to get through the lunch line. She wanted to know why I didn't have any food. I explained what had happened and she gave me some money.

I don't know Patty all that well. We've sat at the same table most of the year, but at opposite ends. We haven't talked much together.

It was really nice of her to loan me the money, Lord. I'm glad I didn't have to do without that pizza and tossed salad while the others around me were eating.

Thank you for taking care of me in such a simple way, Lord. Thank you for helping Patty and me get to know each other better. I think we're going to be good friends.

Does everyone have a boyfriend but me, Lord?

I s there something wrong with me? Is my personality so bad? Do my clothes not look right? Is my face too ugly, or do I look like a little girl? Why don't the boys notice me?

My parents say I can't date until I'm in high school, and I don't have time to talk on the phone all evening with a boy.

But it would be nice not to have the time to answer a phone call or not to be allowed to date instead of not having anyone at all interested in me.

I think that was why Debbie and Cindy got to be such good friends. They both have boyfriends and talk about boys together on the phone. They just have a lot in common.

Who would want to talk to me about their science fair project when they could talk to another girl about what to wear so some boy or other would notice them?

It's not that I want their boyfriends, Lord, or that I know anyone I want for a boyfriend. It's just the principle of the thing.

You understand. I want to be wanted as a girlfriend. I want to be cared for. I want a boy to think I'm important in his life. I want to be like the other girls.

Lord, they pick on me because I'm a Christian

I've never been one to keep my mouth shut. I tell people what I think, so my friends all know that I'm a Christian. It just comes out in the way I think about things and respond to situations.

Most of the time they don't say much. Oh, there are a few boys who like to make comments they know will embarrass me, under their breath, while the teacher is talking about something else. There are times when the group stops telling a joke because I walk up, and they know I wouldn't approve. There are places I'm not invited, and people who don't bother getting to know me because my reputation is "too good."

What really hurts, though, is when there doesn't seem to be much going on and someone starts on a subject they know I feel strongly about. Then they change sides and twist what I've said, and tell me when I'm angry and exasperated, "I thought you were a Christian, Emily. Christians don't lose their temper!"

Oh, Lord, help me not to lose my temper when they try to goad me. Are they really doing it to bother me, or are they testing to see if Christianity would work for them—if it really is the best way to be?

It's hard to witness to the people who see me every day. They know my faults and what I've said I stand for. Help me to live what I believe, Lord.

Junior high's a jungle, Lord

Old people get a gleam in their eye when they hear I'm in junior high.... "Growing up now, aren't you?"... "Best time of your life!" ... "I remember those football games and pizza parties...." They remember the good parts and forget what it's like every day, day to day, in junior high.

Besides the hard work and having so many teachers, besides nobody really knowing who you are, besides having to ride the bus and having to listen to the garbage coming out of so many mouths—it's a jungle full of strange and wild and frightened kids.

There are those of us who are trying out our grown-up ideas and are wondering if they are true. There are those of us who are afraid of growing up and so lash out and say hurtful things to each other. There are those who just hide away in the back of classrooms and buses, too afraid to come out and try junior high life.

The place is new, the schedule is new, the teachers are new, and the classmates are new. There are so many things we don't know and are having to learn—fast. It's a big and colorful and strange experience, Lord, and I wonder if some kids get lost in the jungle.

Help me to search out others who are trying to get through the year. Help me to know what to say and what to do to make their year easier. It's frightening to be lost and alone.

Lord, Mary and I share a music stand

There isn't any other way we are alike that I can see except that we both play cello.

Mary is on the basketball team. She has a boyfriend. She lives in a rich neighborhood and has fabulous clothes. She doesn't make as good grades as I do, but she gets by.

We just aren't very much alike.

But we do love music, and we do think the cello has the best sound of any of the stringed instruments. We like the challenge of solving a new piece of music, and we encourage each other when one of us makes a mistake.

There isn't much time to talk in orchestra. Even when we are having a concert and waiting for our turn to play, we are going over the music, making sure that we can do everything perfectly.

It's funny that I feel so good about Mary. We shouldn't be friends at all, but I feel she is my friend in a special way. We're part of a pair. We go together as a team within the total group. It's hard to explain, but I'm glad we've shared our music stand this year.

Thank you for helping me know someone so different from me, Lord. If we hadn't been in orchestra together, we probably wouldn't have met at all. Thank you for special friends in special places.

◆◆◆

People don't know how hard I work, Lord

Report cards came out today at the end of school. I got on the bus, and someone said, "Emily doesn't even have to look in the envelope—she has all A's again!"

That really burned me up.

They could have good grades too if they worked as hard as I do.

I don't spend all evening watching television. I don't even read mystery stories any more except sometimes on weekends. I don't always go to youth group or youth choir because I have homework, and I spend a lot of time doing research at the library.

It takes more than brains to get good grades, Lord. It takes concentration and giving up some fun time.

I know that some people put in as many hours as I do and really try but still don't get good grades. I'm sorry for them, and I'm thankful that I have a good mind. But most of those who give me a hard time are the ones who don't care anything about studying until the night before a test or a report is due. They're the ones who think I get good grades by good luck.

Help me always to use my mind to serve you, Lord. Help me always to want to learn the most that I can learn and do my assignments to the best of my ability. I'm proud of my grades, and I hope you are proud of me.

Mom says I should give people a chance, Lord

She says I am too judgmental—that I'm too critical of those who aren't like me.

Mom says that I turn people off because I expect more than they are able to give, that they think I won't ever make allowances for their mistakes.

Am I really being that hard to get along with, Lord? Is that why I don't have many friends? Do I expect so much of them that they give up trying to please me?

When I do something wrong, I feel like a nobody, a failure. Am I making other people feel unimportant because they don't reach my standards?

I want to do what is right. I want to stand up for what I believe, Lord, but help me to be understanding too.

Jesus worked among people who were considered terrible sinners, but he loved them. He loved them into being better people. He believed in them and helped them change and believe in themselves.

Where I am too hard on people, Lord, help me change. Help me to accept them as they are without giving up my own beliefs and standards. Help me to be more like Jesus, Lord, when I'm with my friends.

◆◆◆

Lord, I met a new girl at lunch today

You know, when I first had the misunderstanding with Debbie and Cindy, I thought that you would just take care of it and make us all friends again. I thought maybe you would make Debbie like ME again and stop liking Cindy.

But you don't work that way, do you?

I've tried to be nice to them. I even still sit at the same lunch table with them. I talk to them about schoolwork and smile, but things aren't the same.

I've been lonely.

Then today Martha came to school for the first time. Her dad was transferred from out of state, and she has had to leave her home and school and friends. She's been pretty upset.

We began talking in the cafeteria line and discovered that we like some of the same music, books, and games. She's an honor student too, and wants to know where the public library is. And, best of all, we belong to the same church. She's going to come to youth choir with me next week and to youth group.

I've lost a best friend, but it looks like I have another one coming along. Thank you for Martha, Lord. I want to help her get over being sad from moving here. I want her to feel like she belongs. I want to help her be as happy that she's met me as I am that I've met her.

◆◆◆

*How blest are those who know their need
   of God;*
   the kingdom of Heaven is theirs.
How blest are the sorrowful;
   they shall find consolation.
How blest are those of a gentle spirit;
   *they shall have the earth for their
      possession.*
How blest are those who hunger and thirst
   to see right prevail;
   they shall be satisfied.
How blest are those who show mercy;
   mercy shall be shown to them.
How blest are those whose hearts are pure;
   they shall see God.
How blest are the peacemakers;
   God shall call them his sons.
How blest are those who have suffered
   persecution for the cause of right;
   the kingdom of Heaven is theirs.

—Matthew 5:3-10

J U N E . . .

I just looked in the mirror, Lord

I try to stay away from mirrors as much as possible, but when I brush my teeth or comb my hair, I automatically look at myself. There they are . . . an acre of pimples on my forehead and nose . . . shiny, pink, puffy, putrid pimples.

I hate them.

I know, they're part of growing up. All of the beautiful movie stars had pimples when they were young. All of the scientists and politicans and great writers had pimples. I will outgrow them.

I know, eat a well-balanced diet without too many greasy foods, get plenty of rest, keep my face clean. . . .

I know, I know, I know!

But I still hate them. I'm no raving beauty in the first place, so I don't need anything else to make me ugly.

Most of the time I forget that they're there. I talk to people and go places and feel like everyone else. Then I look in the mirror and remember how terrible my pimples look to everyone I meet. It makes me want to stay home in my room so I won't have to face people with a broken out, splotchy forehead and nose.

Help me to forget about the mirror, Lord. Help me to go on with life and remember all of those gorgeous and famous people who survived having pimples. Help me to get over this as quickly as possible.

♦♦♦

Maybe I've been too worried about grades, Lord

We got back a math test today. I was really upset because the teacher had marked a problem wrong that was right. Mr. Rogerson went over the test with us, and I saw that he had graded my paper wrong. I went right up to him to have him change the grade.

He laughed and said, "I'm sorry, Emily. You should have gotten a 102% instead of a 98%. Didn't mean to wreck your average."

I got to thinking this afternoon—what's the difference in a few numbers? An "A" is an "A."

Then I remembered how happy Sue was to get her "C." Sue had worked really hard, but she just didn't understand what Mr. Rogerson was teaching us. Then, the day before the test she started to see what he meant. She was *thankful* for a "C"—I would have been carrying on, crying, and hurt if I'd gotten a "C."

Lord, thank you for my ability to learn. Help me to find pleasure in the learning and not to be so concerned with the grades I get. Help me to be more humble about my test scores, more eager to help others work through assignments they don't understand.

◆◆◆

My science teacher understands me, Lord

We went on an all-day field trip to the state university today for a statewide science competition. The school bus was full, and Miss Simmons sat by me on the way back home.

She's always been helpful in class, and she sure knows her subject. She's an interesting teacher, but I didn't know her as a person until today.

Miss Simmons is really a good listener. Well, we had a long time to talk. First we talked about the exhibit today and then about what we'd been studying together. Then she told me about her days in college, and I told her about wanting to be a research scientist when I get out of school.

I don't know exactly when we started talking about it, but I told her about having trouble with Cindy and Debbie, and the kids teasing me about my grades and my Christian beliefs.

She really understood what I've been going through. She told me about her time in junior high. She said she was a lot like me.

Lord, I hope I grow up to be as nice as Miss Simmons. I wouldn't want to be just like her—I'm myself—but I hope I'll be a good listener if someone wants to share with me. Thank you for my science teacher, Lord.

♦♦♦

Lord, I'm not any taller

They measured us in p.e. today for the end of the year records. I cannot believe it. I thought I would have grown an inch at least!

Mom's grandmothers were both under five feet tall, and so was Dad's mother. But their dads and granddads were all over six feet tall.

What happened to me?

This heredity business is scary.

What if I never get any taller? I'll be a midget! I'll have to buy my clothes in the children's department of the store.

Everyone else in class grew at least an inch since September—two girls grew almost three inches this year.

My sister is growing fast and so is my brother. What if they get taller than I am? That would be humiliating . . . my little sister, two years younger, taller than me!

Lord, I really want to get taller. I know that the Scripture says we can't get taller by worrying about it, but it IS a worry. I don't want to be six feet tall like my grandfather, but I sure would like to grow a few more inches.

Help me to be patient, Lord, and help me to be as satisfied with my body as I am with my mind.

I wasn't invited, Lord

Last fall, when Debbie and I were still best friends, her mother told us we could have an end-of-the-year party at their house. We started planning what we would do and who we would invite. We thought about what fun we would have getting together to decorate and make the food.

The party is tonight, Lord.

They were talking about it at the lunch table today—what they would wear, and who was coming, and how late they would get to stay up because they're in junior high now.

Mostly Cindy and Debbie were talking, but three or four of the other girls put in their ideas. Right in front of me!

I wasn't invited.

It was almost like they were doing it in my presence to hurt me. Why? Why do they want to hurt me, Lord?

I've really tried to be friends this year. I haven't said anything ugly about them even when they were being mean to me.

If I had been invited, if I *had* gone to their party, I probably wouldn't have had a great time. I might not have even gone, but it would have been nice to have been invited.

Lord, it hurts when people let me down. It hurts when I don't know why people don't like me. It hurts when it all seems to be on purpose. I wish it didn't hurt so much.

♦♦♦

Lord, I can do a history definition in 5 minutes now!

Do you remember those nights last fall and winter when I *slaved* over my history homework? It took me 20 minutes to get through the material, pick out the answers, think about what I wanted to say, and write out a definition.

I must have gotten better organized—I have just finished an assignment of ten definitions in less than an hour!

It must come with experience, with trying to find the right way to do research in the textbook. Maybe I just think differently about history now and can see the relationships Miss Morris is after.

Whatever it is, it sure is wonderful to have a little free time in the evenings.

It seems easier to get all of my assignments done now, and I don't have to spend so much time studying for tests. I seem to know which information is important and which is just "interesting on the side."

Thank you for helping me stick to my work long enough and hard enough to develop some good study habits, Lord. It was really discouraging on those nights when it seemed all I did was come home from school, study, eat, and sleep. I'm glad those nights are over.

Lord, school isn't everything

I've been so uptight about my first year in junior high that I guess I've sort of ignored what else is happening in my life. My family, my church, my community are all special to me, and this *has* been a good year.

My dad has helped me practice batting a ball better. My sister and I have gone on long bike rides. Mom's teaching me to use the sewing machine. My brother and I set up a family art gallery, and we've been doing some cooking together—sometimes making dessert, sometimes a whole meal.

Our youth group is so much fun. We've had picnics, retreats, special studies about world hunger, death, and drug abuse. We've planned community projects to help shut-ins get their leaves raked, and to distribute food, clothing, and toys. We've had Bible studies and sleep overs and we've collected money for the homeless. We feel like we are making our world a better place.

The fireman's parade, community Halloween party, Christmas caroling down Main Street, ice skating at Hirshman's pond—my town is a terrific place to grow up, Lord. Thank you for putting me here in my town, in my church, in my family.

Thank you for giving me other things to do and places to go besides school. I know these are the years for me to study to fulfill that special purpose you have for me in the world. But thanks for those other places where I'm learning to be me, too. It's a beautiful life you've given me, Lord.

Next year has to be better, Lord

I'll know how to open my locker in the middle of a noisy crowd. I'll know what to wear and how to get to class *fast*. I'll know more people in all of my classes right from the start, and some of the teachers and workers at school will know me.

It really was hard beginning last September, Lord. It was scary to know so little about my new school and teachers and work.

I think I know myself better now too. I know that I *can* learn to work faster. I *can* make new friends. I *can* survive if I forget my lunch money or miss the bus.

I know next year will be hard in new ways, Lord. It wouldn't be a challenge if it weren't different, but I know that I can handle it . . . with your help.

Thanks for being there *every* time I needed you this year. Thanks for listening to the silly worries as well as the real ones. Thanks for helping me see when *I* needed to change more than the people I wanted to change.

Growing up is hard, but you make it easier. Thanks.

Lord, help me find people who are hurting

I know how it hurts to lose a friend. I know how it hurts to think there's no one special to listen to me.

I know that there are new friends to be found—sometimes among people I hadn't suspected were such good prospects.

So many kids are afraid to search out new friends. Maybe *they're* new in school. Maybe *they're* sure no one will want to be their friend. Maybe *they're* just shy.

I want to set a goal for next year to be a friend to those who are hurting.

I don't mean some crusade to help all of the helpless. That sounds a little fakey to me, and I sure wouldn't have the time to take on the whole school. But little by little, as I go through each day, help me look for the people who need a listener. Help me be the friend someone needs when that person gets a bad grade on a test or doesn't get invited or doesn't make the team.

I guess I've expected it all to come *to me* this year—people to fall over themselves wanting to be *my* friend. Help me to look for those who need a friend and be their friend next year, Lord. Help me heal a little of the hurting.

◆◆◆

There are clearings in the jungle, Lord

My eyes are seeing through the blur a little better now. I guess I'd been thinking mostly of the bad and scary things in junior high.

There's still that terrible language in the halls and classrooms and buses. There are still lots of people who don't know each other, long nights of homework, and teachers who seem to know just when to give a test—when two other teachers have assigned one.

But I see some clearings in the jungle, Lord!

I see teachers who really do care—teachers who will take time to listen if I take time to talk to them. I see people who share lunch money and invite new kids to sit with them. I see ninth-graders who pick up seventh-graders from the steps, and bus drivers who help get cellos unstuck. I see kids who are excited when others make the honor roll, and those who play just as hard when they're put on the second-string team.

There are many things I would like to change about junior high to make it a better place, and many things I cannot change at all. Do you feel that way about your world, Lord? It could be so much better if we *all* were Christian—but there are special people and places making things better. There *are* clearings in the jungle.

Thank you, Lord, for showing me some of the good things in my world and yours. Thank you for hope in the present and for the future.

*B*ut when you pray, go into a room by yourself, shut the door, and pray to your Father who is there in the secret place; and your Father who sees what is secret will reward you.

—Matthew 6:6

MY MONTHLY PRAYER DIARY. . .

A U G U S T . . .

"Set your mind on God's kingdom and his justice before everything else, and all the rest will come to you as well."

—Matthew 6:33

My concerns and commitments . . .

AUGUST

SEPTEMBER . . .

"So do not be anxious about tomorrow; tomorrow will look after itself. Each day has troubles enough of its own."

—Matthew 6:34

My concerns and commitments . . .

SEPTEMBER

O C T O B E R . . .

"How blest are those who know their need of God; the kingdom of heaven is theirs."

—Matthew 5:3

◆◆◆

My concerns and commitments . . .

OCTOBER

NOVEMBER . . .

"How blest are the sorrowful; they shall find consolation."

—Matthew 5:4

◆◆◆

My concerns and commitments . . .

N O V E M B E R

DECEMBER . . .

"How blest are the peacemakers; God shall call them his sons."

—Matthew 5:9

◆◆◆

My concerns and commitments . . .

DECEMBER

JANUARY . . .

"How blest are those of a gentle spirit; they shall have the earth for their possession."

—Matthew 5:5

◆◆◆

My concerns and commitments . . .

JANUARY

FEBRUARY . . .

"How blest are those who hunger and thirst to see right prevail; they shall be satisfied."

—Matthew 5:6

My concerns and commitments . . .

FEBRUARY

M A R C H . . .

*"How blest are those who show mercy;
mercy shall be shown to them."*

—Matthew 5:7

◆◆◆

My concerns and commitments . . .

MARCH

APRIL...

"How blest are those whose hearts are pure; they shall see God."

—Matthew 5:8

◆◆◆

My concerns and commitments . . .

APRIL

MAY . . .

"And you, like the lamp, must shed light among your fellows, so that, when they see the good you do, they may give praise to your Father in heaven."

—Matthew 5:16

My concerns and commitments . . .

M A Y

J U N E...

"For everyone who asks receives, he who seeks finds, and to him who knocks, the door will be opened."

—Matthew 7:8

My plans for making
next year better . . .

Remember, God wants to share your life with you—the problems and worries and the special good feelings. You can talk to him in prayer wherever you are, whenever you want. God is always there with you.

The Author

Born in Washington, D.C., Clair Cosby grew up as an only child in that city and its Virginia suburbs. Her father died when she was nine years old; her mother remarried when Clair was twelve. Clair graduated from Mary Washington College in Fredericksburg, Virginia, with a B.A. in English and French. She has completed 33 graduate hours  in the field of learning disabilities from the University of Virginia, James Madison University, and George Mason University.

Virginia State Vice-President of the Future Teachers of America in high school, Clair has enjoyed her years in the teaching profession. She has taught junior high English and educable mentally retarded, learning disabled, and emotionally disturbed students ranging in age from seven through eighteen. She is currently a special education resource teacher.

Clair is married to J. Mason Cosby, pastor of the Burke United Methodist Church, Burke, Virginia. The Cosbys have three children: Sarah, Sallie, and James.

Actively involved in church work all her life, Clair has led and been a member of choirs, church school classes, prayer and missionary groups, and she has established and worked on many church newsletters. Especially enjoying work with the church school, she has developed a series of teaching enrichment seminars for local churches and has taught in children, youth, and adult divisions for more than 20 years.

Clair says, "I wrote *Junior High's a Jungle, Lord* when our first daughter had just gone through the transition from elementary school to junior high. She's survived that wonderful-terrible, exciting-scary, rewarding-frustrating seventh-grade year, and this year my second daughter will be facing similar experiences."

Clair is looking forward to continuing her writing ministry, sharing the good news of Jesus Christ as an outgrowth of her daily personal adventure with God.